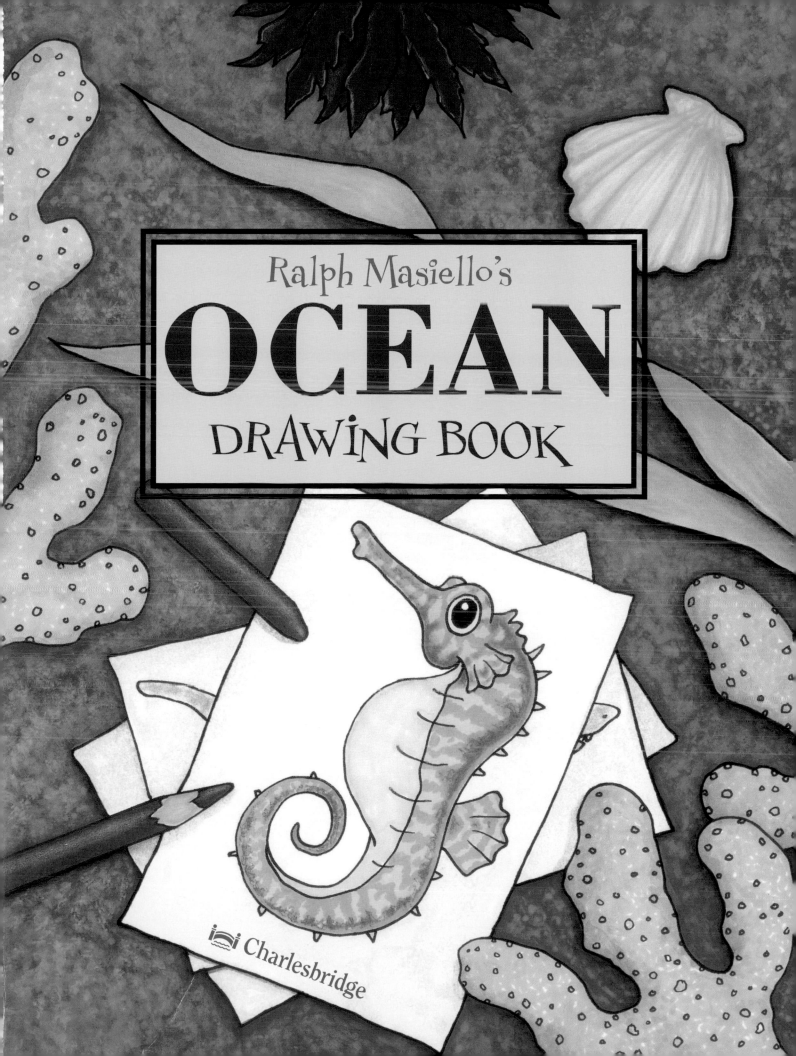

To my mom, Grace, who lives her name so well—R. M.

Also in this series:
Ralph Masiello's Bug Drawing Book
Ralph Masiello's Dinosaur Drawing Book

Other books illustrated by Ralph Masiello:
The Dinosaur Alphabet Book
The Extinct Alphabet Book
The Flag We Love
The Frog Alphabet Book
The Icky Bug Alphabet Book
The Icky Bug Counting Book
The Skull Alphabet Book
The Yucky Reptile Alphabet Book
Cuenta los insectos

Published by Charlesbridge
85 Main Street
Watertown, MA 02472
(617) 926-0329
www.charlesbridge.com

Library of Congress Cataloging-in-Publication Data
Masiello, Ralph.
[Ocean drawing book]
Ralph Masiello's ocean drawing book.
p. cm.
ISBN-13: 978-1-57091-529-1; ISBN-10: 1-57091-529-6 (reinforced for library use)
ISBN-13: 978-1-57091-530-7; ISBN-10: 1-57091-530-X (softcover)
1. Marine animals in art—Juvenile literature. 2. Drawing—Technique—Juvenile
literature. I. Title.
NC781.M37 2006
743.6'177—dc22   2005019968

Printed in China
(hc) 10 9 8 7 6 5 4 3 2 1
(sc) 10 9 8 7 6 5 4 3 2 1

Illustrations done in mixed media
Display type set in Couchlover, designed by Chank, Minneapolis, MN;
text type set in Goudy
Color separations by Chroma Graphics, Singapore
Printed and bound by Jade Productions
Production supervision by Brian G. Walker
Designed by Susan Mallory Sherman

Hello, Fellow Artists!

I love the ocean! I've been illustrating books since 1985. However, before going to art school I studied marine biology (the science of ocean life). I have dived with sharks, moray eels, whales, and dolphins, as well as many other incredible ocean creatures. There is an amazing, beautiful, and mysterious world beneath the waves—and with practice and patience you can bring it to the surface in your drawings.

For this book I chose some of the ocean life that kids I have met enjoy drawing. Follow the red steps to create these interesting creatures and their surroundings. Then color them in using your favorite artist's tools. You'll also find some blue extra challenge boxes to liven up your creations. I hope you enjoy drawing as much as I do!

Happy drawing, *Ralph*

Choose your tools

pastel pencil · crayon · watercolor · fine-tip marker · colored pencil · marker · poster paint

Clams

Closed

Open

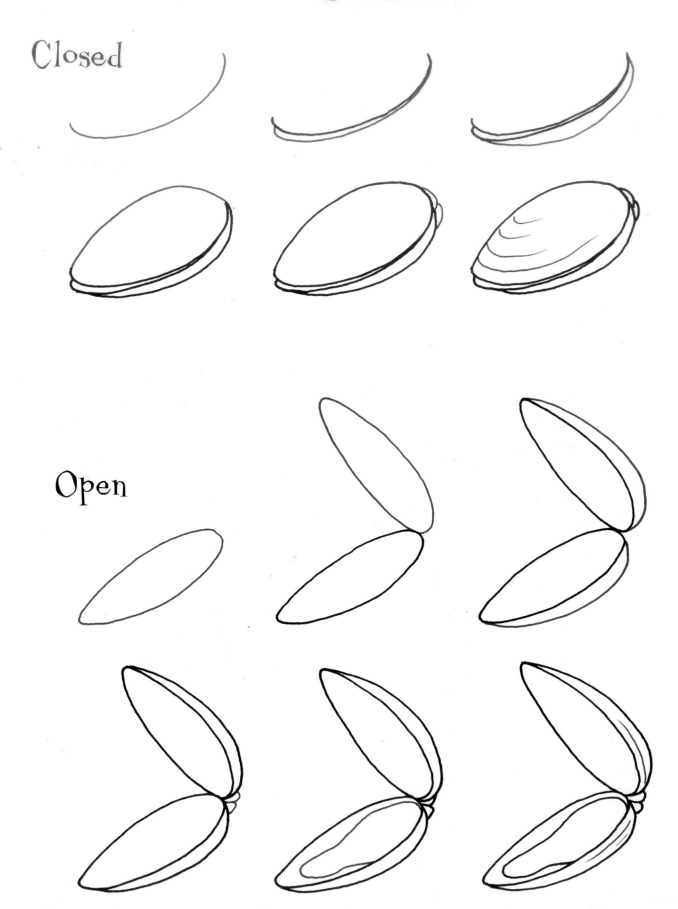

Here's a cluster of clams.

crayon

Starfish (Sea star)

Seashells

Drawing will make you a star!

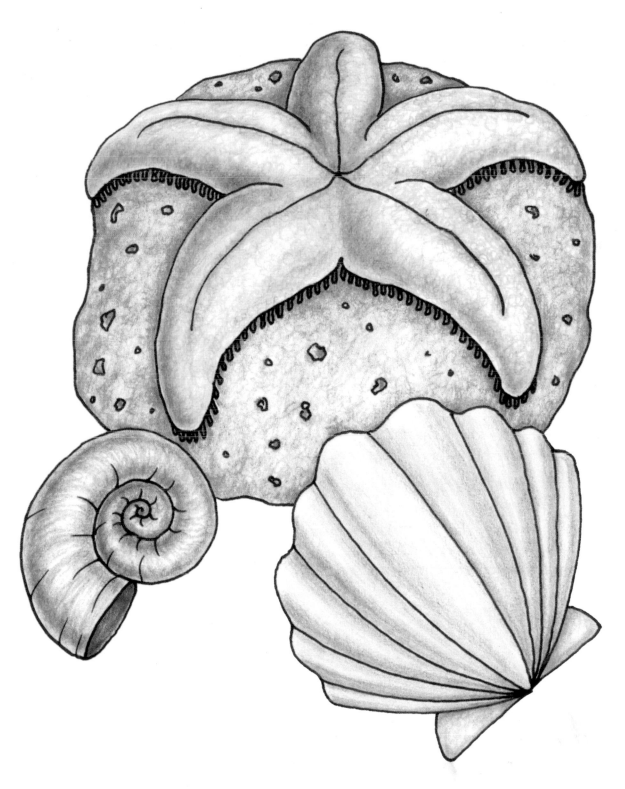

colored pencil

Clownfish

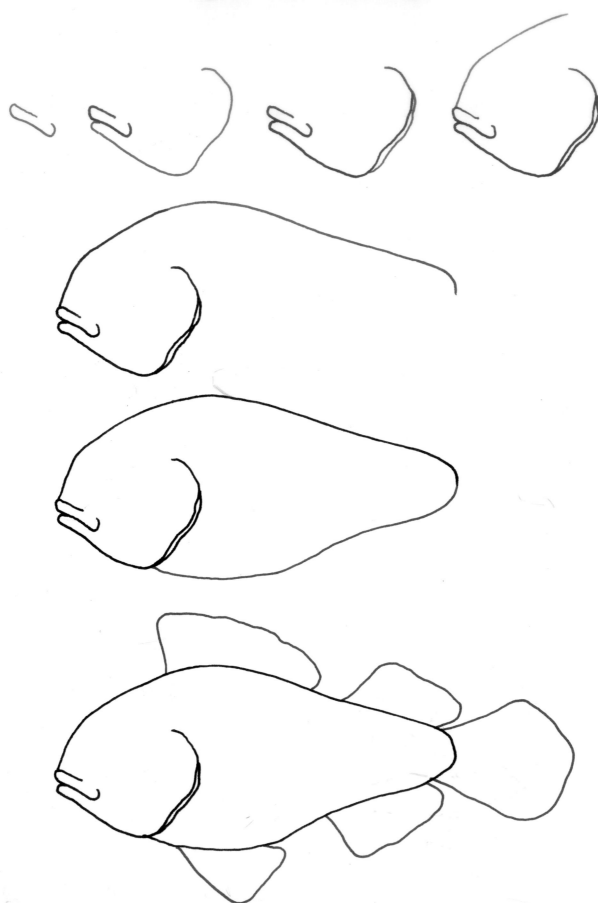

Anemone

Who's that clowning around?

watercolor

Dolphin

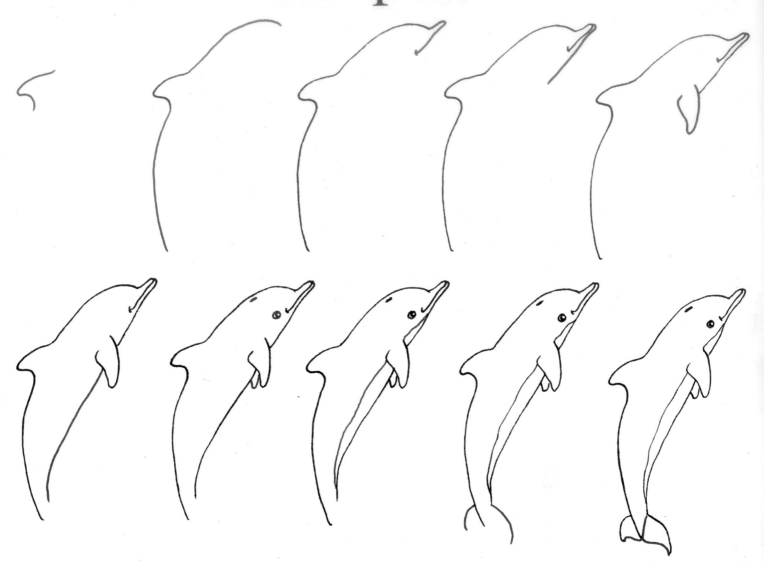

Splashes

Water

Make your dolphin jump.

Splish, splash!

pastel pencil

Seaweed

Kelp

Green Seaweed

Red Seaweed

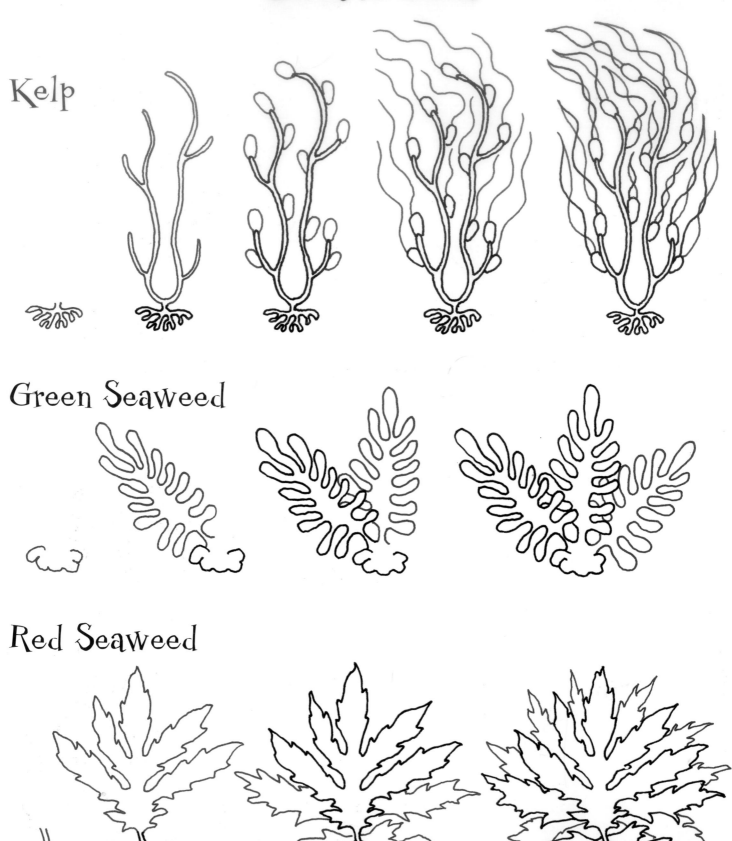

Coral

Stag Coral

Brain Coral

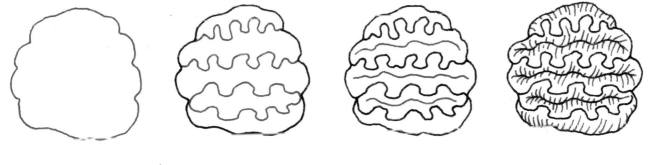

Fan Coral

Sea Horse

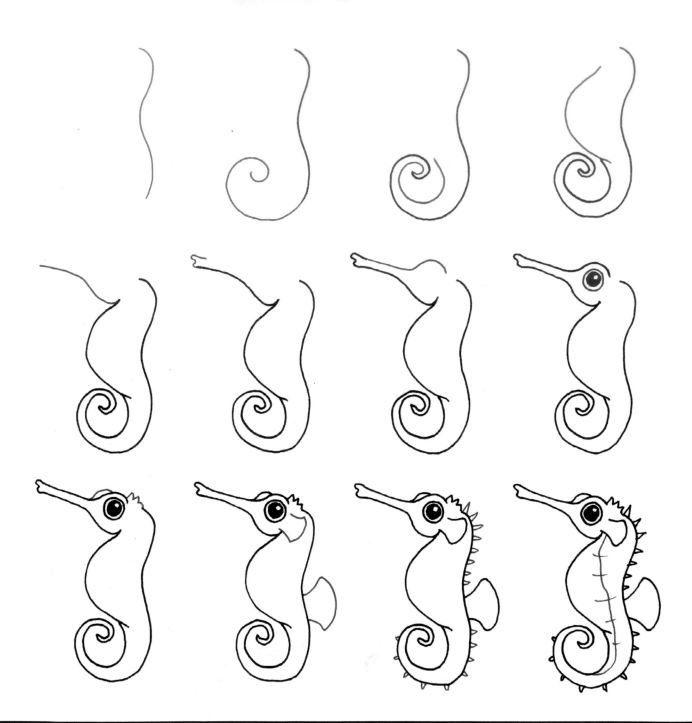

Realistic Fin

Saddle up!

fine-tip marker

Squid

Suction Cups

Twist those tentacles!

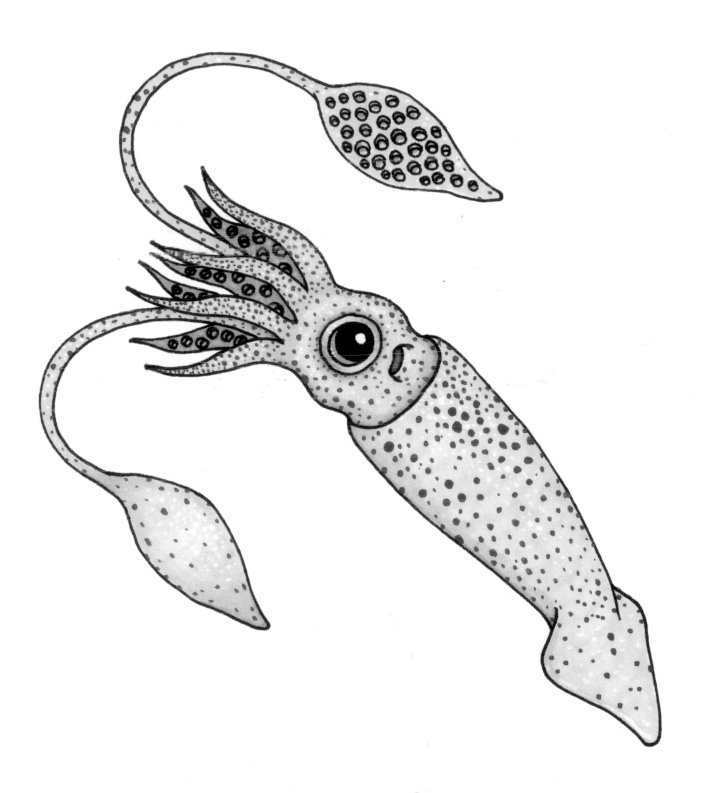

marker and poster paint

Moray Eel

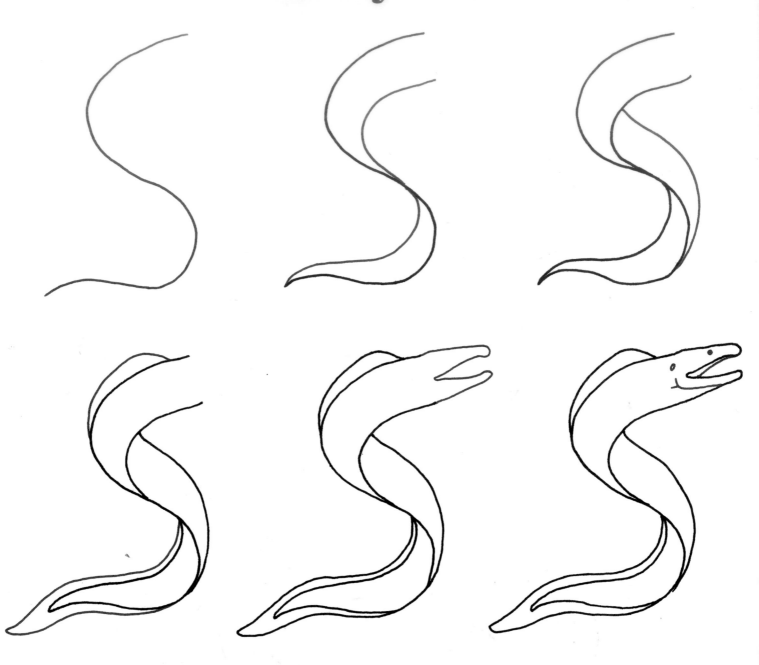

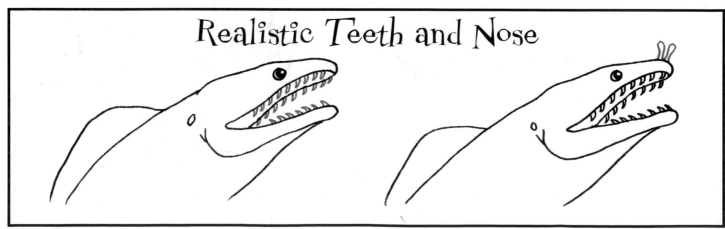

Realistic Teeth and Nose

Sneaky, sneaky! Watch out for Mr. Moray!

marker and watercolor

Shark

There are many different sharks, and they come in a variety of sizes and shapes. Here are some I think are cool:

Mackerel Shark
"Great White"

Thresher Shark

Tiger Shark

Basking Shark

Sandbar Shark

Nurse Shark

Humpback Whale

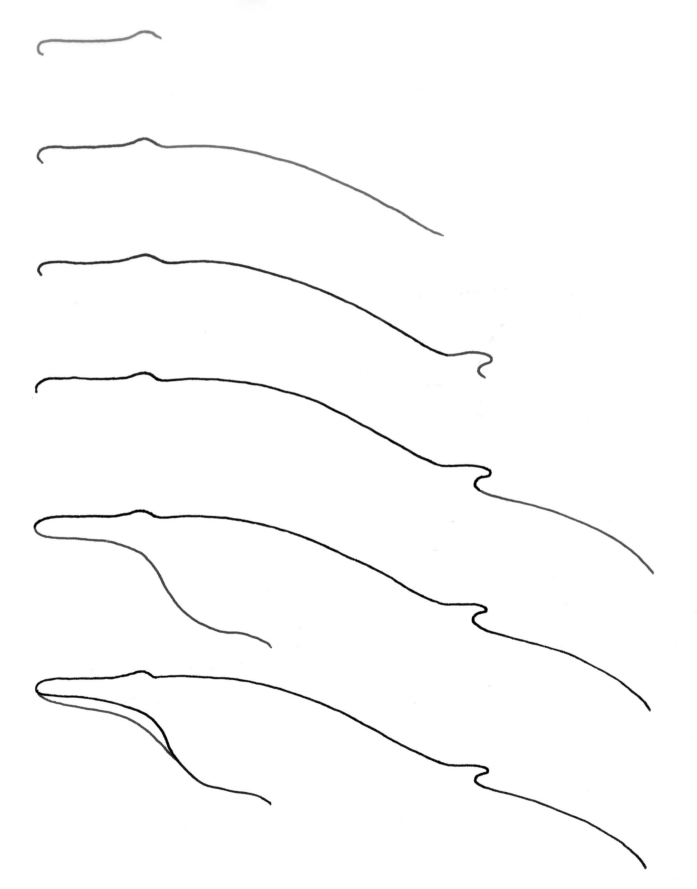

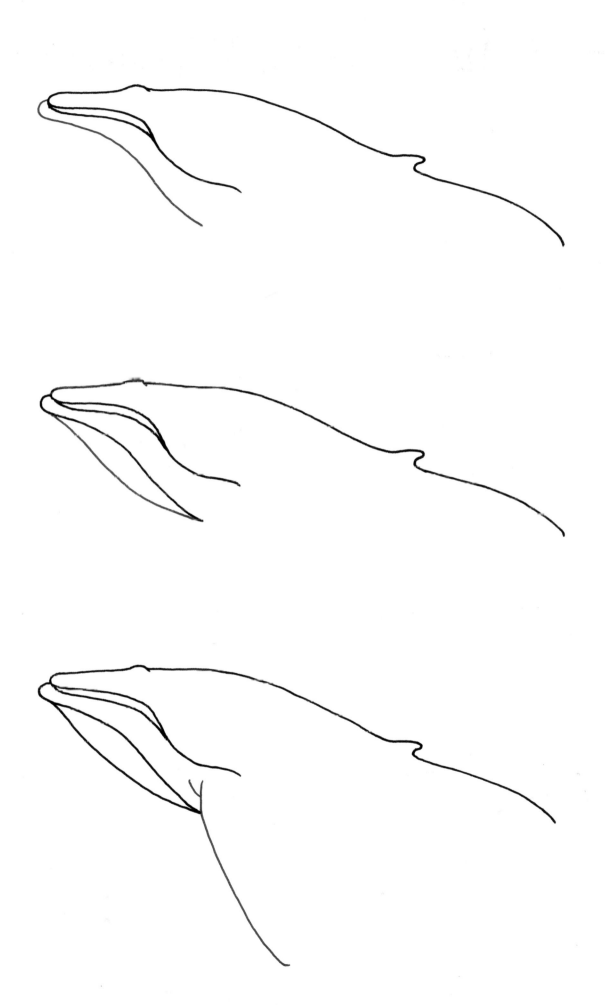

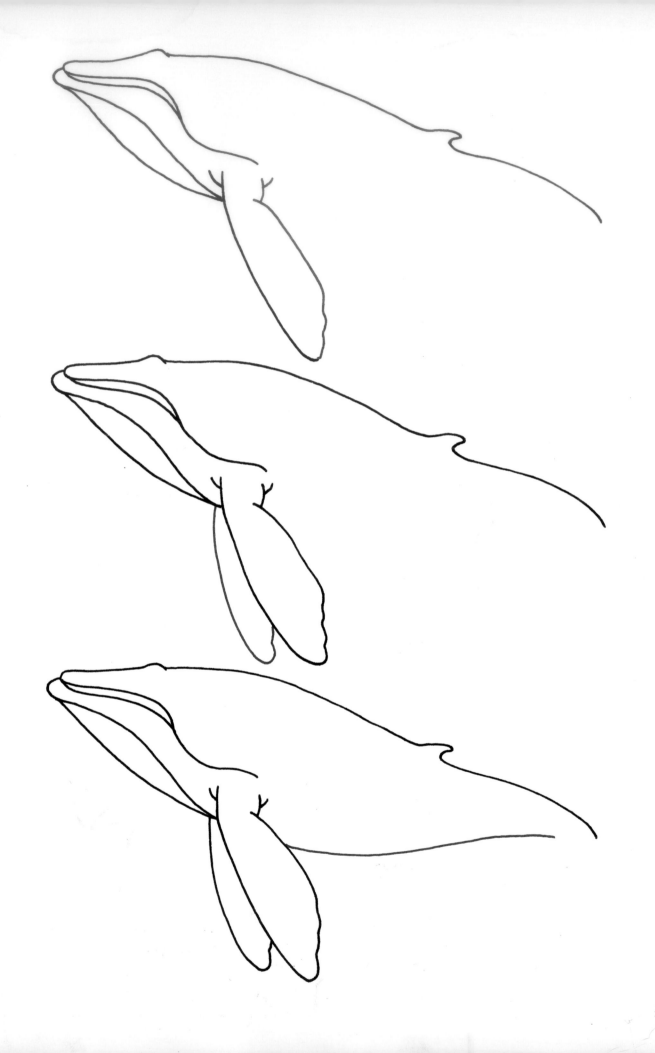

Barnacles

Drawing is a whale of a good time!

Time to get a wee bit wacky!
Use your imagination.

Now that you know how to dive into ocean drawings, it's time to create your own imaginary ocean life forms. Use what you've learned and create something new and unique. Here's a creature I made called the "Shark-hors-phin."

Have fun, and keep those drawings flowing!